Original title:
Heather Hymns

Copyright © 2025 Creative Arts Management OÜ
All rights reserved.

Author: Maya Livingston
ISBN HARDBACK: 978-1-80566-758-2
ISBN PAPERBACK: 978-1-80566-828-2

Verses Beneath the Blooming Sky

In fields so bright, the flowers sway,
A bee took my snack—how rude, I say!
With petals dancing, they mock my stride,
While I trip over roots, in laughter I hide.

The sun shines down, the clouds all grin,
A rabbit hops by, thinking it's thin.
I join the chorus of giggles and glee,
Nature's the comedian, just look and see!

Chanting in the Rustic Fields

Amidst the blooms, a rooster crowed,
Singing off-key, it can't hit the road!
What a duet with sheep and the breeze,
A cacophony of nature's unease.

With daisies and clover, we all take a bow,
A squirrel steals my lunch—don't know how!
While I laugh at the circus, the daisies all cheer,
Nature's comedy show, we hold so dear!

Ode to the Resilient Flower

A flower stands tall, despite the bugs,
But ants hold a party and give me shrugs.
They dance on the petals, a wild parade,
I watch from the sidelines, all plans delayed.

With roots dug deep, it faces the storm,
But oh! The wind gives its style a new form.
It bends and it bows, like a jester in jest,
In the garden's grand show, it knows it's the best!

Ballad of the Wind-Swept Moor

Upon the moor, the heather flirts,
With breezes that tease, in quirky shirts.
A sheep in a cap, oh what a sight!
Wobbling along, it thinks it's polite.

The wind is a prankster, playing its tune,
Whisking my hat away—oh, what a boon!
I chase after laughter, through tussocks and foam,
On a merry-go-round, I'll call this place home!

Dawn Chorus of the Heather Fields

The birds wake up to sing their tune,
While cows jump over the bright baboon.
Grasshoppers dance in a silly way,
As flowers giggle to greet the day.

A rooster crows, then takes a nap,
While sheep play poker, what a trap!
The sun spills laughter over the hills,
And ants don hats for their morning thrills.

A chatty squirrel steals a berry,
While a snail drags on, never in a hurry.
With each note, the fields come alive,
As laughter and joy start to arrive.

So join the chorus, let's make some noise,
In heather fields where life enjoys.
We'll sing and dance, all day long,
In nature's symphony, oh so strong!

The Language of Lavender

In fields of purple, secrets unfold,
Lavender whispers, bold yet controlled.
The bees confer in a busy chat,
While butterflies giggle, 'Where's our mat?'

One flower says, 'I'm tickled pink!'
Another replies, 'I can hardly think!'
The breeze carries tales of charm and cheer,
As the colors converse, oh so clear.

A ladybug rolls on to find some fun,
While moths have meetings, planning to run.
The air is filled with tea party grins,
As laughter blooms where friendship begins.

So come and listen to the floral jest,
In lavender fields, we're truly blessed.
With petals twirling, we'll share a laugh,
In this garden of giggles, we'll have a blast!

Twilight Reveries of the Glen

As day fades out, the critters appear,
The glowworms wiggle, 'Come have some cheer!'
The owls hoot jokes, as bats take a spin,
While hedgehogs gather for a silly grin.

The clouds wear pajamas, fluffy and light,
While fireflies dance, flashing with delight.
'What's for dinner?' a fox makes a fuss,
'A pie of stars, just for us!'

The brook chuckles softly, with ripples so bright,
As frogs croon songs to the moon's silver light.
The night is young, with a whimsical air,
In this twilight glen, nothing can compare.

So let's paint the night with laughter and glee,
In this magical place, just you and me.
With dreams that sparkle as we sway,
We'll dance with shadows till the break of day!

Heartbeats of the Briar

In the briar patch, a party ignites,
Rabbits are waltzing, oh what delights!
A hedgehog spills juice from his cup,
While crickets leap and start to hop.

Thorns roll their eyes at the clumsy show,
'Keep it down, will ya? We don't want the crow!'
But laughter erupts, a sound so sweet,
As badgers join in on their little feet.

Tulips chuckle, swaying along,
'The briar's alive with a joyful song!'
The sun dips low in a crimson sky,
While whispers of giggles float by and by.

So if you're lost near the tangled vine,
Just follow the chuckles, it'll be fine.
In the heart of the briar, fun never tires,
Where every heartbeat fuels laughter's fires!

Whispers in the Wild

In the glen where the rabbits play,
Squirrels chatter all through the day,
A hedgehog winks with a cheeky grin,
He finally found his way back in!

The badger struts, so proud and bold,
Telling tales of treasures untold,
But all he found was an old lost shoe,
He's convinced it's worth a fortune too!

The birds sit perched, with taunts and jeers,
Mocking the deer who sips his beers,
A stag with a crown, just full of pride,
Stumbles over his own hefty side!

Yet here we laugh, in nature's throng,
With silly stories, where we belong,
In every rustle, and chirp, and breeze,
Wild whispers tickle our hearts with ease!

Echoes of the Moorland

On the moors where the sheep all roam,
A ram declares this land his home,
With puffs of wool and a haughty air,
He thinks that he is quite the rare!

A fox sneaks by with a crafty plan,
To steal some lunch from the silly man,
But ends up caught in a tangle of bramble,
His escape turns into quite a scramble!

The puddles reflect the sky's blue hue,
While a crow laughs at a wee lost shoe,
'Fashionable yellow!' he caws with glee,
'That's so last year! You can't fool me!'

Yet amidst the chaos, a joy unfolds,
With laughter ringing, as life beholds,
In echoes bright, the moorland sings,
Tales of nonsense and silly things!

Songs of the Purple Bloom

In fields adorned with blooms so fine,
A bunny hops, and thinks he'll dine,
But the flowers laugh, 'Not on our watch!'
They spritz him back with a lavender scotch!

A clumsy bee buzzes to take a turn,
Knocking petals down, oh how they spurn!
'You're a disgrace!' the daisies yell,
'Go home, dear friend, you've rung the bell!'

A ladybug sports her fancy spot,
Claiming it's the bestest she's got,
But her friends giggle, with whispers bold,
'It looks like you've been rolled in gold!'

Yet through it all, the colors gleam,
Life's little jokes add to the theme,
With every petal that dances and sways,
Songs of laughter fill our days!

Melodies of the Gorse

On hills where the yellow bushes sway,
A goat sings loudly, come what may,
His bleats echo with such delight,
Even the rabbits join in the fight!

A toad hops in with a trumpeting tune,
Claiming he's the best croaker by noon,
But slips on a rock and lands with a flop,
Now hums a tune that'll never stop!

The hedgehogs are hosting a merry dance,
In polka dots, they prance and prance,
Rolling in circles, then lost in a twist,
Claiming they're stars, can't be missed!

With wind in our hair, we chuckle away,
At the antics played on this bright, sunny day,
In melodies rich, where laughter boasts,
Gorse blooms sing of joy, that's what matters most!

Lullabies from the Rugged Hills

In the hills where the sheep like to bleat,
You may find a goat with two left feet.
Lambs prance around, oh what a sight!
Who knew being clumsy could feel so right!

The wind whispers secrets of woolly delight,
While rabbits attempt to hop, but just slide.
A family of ducks glitter in mud,
And sing when they swim like a bubbly thud!

A fox tries to dance, oh what an affair,
But ends up with twigs and a flower in hair.
Highland cows moo out a catchy tune,
Adding a beat to the afternoon!

So come, hear the giggles of nature's own,
Where laughter and chaos are brightly sewn.
In the rugged hills where the blunders roam,
Lullabies echo, making all feel at home.

Ballad of the Endless Meadow

In the meadow where daisies pop,
A rabbit gets stuck in a cabbage crop.
With a wiggle and jiggle, he'll make a retreat,
But ends up proclaiming defeat with a fleet!

Butterflies dawdle, sipping sweet dew,
While bumblebees hum a curious tune.
Grasshoppers leap, but mostly just fall,
In this realm of laughter, there's fun for us all!

A sheep sings low in a comical key,
Claiming the title of nature's off-key.
Even the daisies bend down with a smile,
At the antics that flourish in this sunny aisle.

So grab a spot on this wide-open land,
Join the frolics, it's perfectly planned!
In the endless meadow, the giggles will swell,
As we dance with the critters, under nature's spell.

Stanzas from the Scot's Glade

In the glade where the trees like to sway,
A squirrel gossips the day away.
With acorns aplenty, it hoards and it stores,
Laughing at passersby, as it roars!

Foxes chase tails, making rounds with flair,
While a badger just sits, with quite the blank stare.
It dreams of cheese, perhaps a nice brie,
Snoring quite loudly, oh look, there's a bee!

A chorus erupts from a perched little bird,
Who thinks it's an opera star, quite absurd!
The otters splash wildly, just for a scene,
Turning the glade into an aquatic dream!

So step into laughter, let nature be loud,
Join the frolicsome creatures; be part of the crowd.
In the Scot's glade, where humor takes flight,
Every rustle of leaves sparks joy and delight.

Poetry of the Verdant Heath

Upon the heath where the flowers do scheme,
A lizard takes naps in a sunbeam's dream.
Doing yoga with bells on its toes,
Wondering why no one ever knows!

A hedgehog rolls round in a curious ball,
Wishing to be the quickest of all.
Yet every attempt ends in quite the mess,
As he tumbles down, and feels the stress!

With thistles that giggle and giggles that chime,
Nature finds ways to express in pure rhyme.
Young storks practice flapping, but much to their shock,
They land in the mud, giving all a great knock!

So relish the moments where folly is king,
And laugh at the creatures who dance and sing.
In the verdant heath, where whimsy abounds,
The joy of the wild in pure laughter resounds.

Nature's Embrace in Bloom

In a garden where flowers laugh,
The daisies dance, a comedy half.
Bees buzzing tunes, so offbeat,
Wiggling their wings, they can't find their feet.

A butterfly slips, oh what a sight,
Spreading its wings, it takes to flight.
But swirls in circles, can't find the way,
Instead, it lands on a daffodil's fray.

The sun sneezes rays, they tickle the air,
While squirrels debate if they really care.
"Why gather nuts?" one throws a fit,
"Let's just play tag, we'll never quit!"

Such joy found in the realm of green,
Where laughter bubbles, happy and keen.
Nature's folly, in colors so bright,
Bringing smiles, from morning to night.

Whispers of the Purple Moor

On the moor where odd things roam,
A rabbit wears glasses, reads at home.
He squints at the text, tilting his head,
"Is that a carrot?" he finally said.

The sheep on the hill hold a voting spree,
"Should we go left or take a tree?"
Debates and baa's fill the sunny air,
Until one trips over without a care.

An owl hoots softly, "What a grand night!"
While foxes play chess, in moon's soft light.
"Checkmate!" one yells, throwing his paw,
The pieces scatter; it's all a raw draw.

Yet laughter echoes in shadows so deep,
Where even the stars seem to giggle and peep.
Nature's quirks, with a twist so grand,
Become silly tales upon the land.

Songs of the Mountain Flower

Up in the hills, where the breeze sings fine,
A flower holds court with humor divine.
"I'm taller than you!" the daisies chime,
"Step back, I'm blooming, it's my time!"

A robin falls asleep in mid-flight,
Lands on a bud—it's a comical sight.
The petals tremble with each little snore,
"Wake up!" they giggle, "We want to explore!"

The mountains chuckle, soft snowflakes fly,
Tickled by whispers from the clouds up high.
"Mushrooms are sprouting a dance party soon,
Join us for laughter under the moon!"

In this land of blooms, all colors unite,
Crafting odd tales that feel just right.
Nature's fun, wrapped in petals so sweet,
A waltz of giggles, a colorful beat.

Twilight Serenade of the Highland

Evening descends with a mischievous glance,
Crickets begin their wacky dance.
They chirp a tune that's all out of beat,
Grasshoppers join in—oh, what a feat!

A deer prances by in the twilight glow,
Tripping on roots, saying, "Oh no, no!"
The bushes all giggle, shake with glee,
Not a care in the world, wild and free.

Stars peek out, giving twinkling winks,
While squirrels hold debates on nuts and drinks.
"Tea or acorns?" they ponder aloud,
A whimsical chat that draws quite a crowd.

In the highlands where the funny finds ground,
Nature's orchestra plays joyfully round.
Melodies burst, filled with pure delight,
As twilight serenades the close of the night.

Ballads of the Red and Purple

In fields where colors dance and sway,
A rabbit wore a floral beret.
He thought he could hop and impress,
But tripped on a twig, oh what a mess!

The bees were buzzing a goofy tune,
While flowers swayed beneath the moon.
A squirrel laughed in the blooming shade,
'You'll never make it, your charm's delayed!'

The daisies shrugged, their petals bright,
'We're all just here for the pure delight.'
A dancing snail joined the parade,
With moves so slick, he truly displayed!

Oh, let's revel in this garden caper,
With laughter that sticks like a table paper.
In shades of red and purple glee,
Nature's jesters, forever free!

Tones of the Flourishing Wilds

The flowers gathered, what a show,
A tulip wore a bright yellow bow.
The daisies giggled, what a sight,
As a worm wobbled, all full of fright!

In meadows where the wild things play,
A goat sang loudly, scaring away.
The bumblebees dropped their sweet treats,
As the goats tap-danced on their own big feet!

A butterfly dressed in stripes and flair,
Tried to impress a lady with care.
But landed right on a muddy spot,
Said "Wow, this date has hit the dot!"

So join the laughter, lend your ear,
To silly songs that bring out cheer.
In flourishing wilds where joy ignites,
Nature sings through the day and nights!

Silent Songs from the Highland

On highland hills where the sheep would roam,
A sheep decided to claim a dome.
But every time it tried to leap,
It landed in a pile of sheep's deep sleep!

The larks sang tunes all twisted and odd,
While a fox played tricks, oh my, how it trod!
The heather swayed to an ancient beat,
As the badger danced on his little two feet.

The sun peeked over with a golden grin,
As the misty valleys let fun begin.
Rabbits pranced, creating a furrow,
Their leaping larks turned heads to follow!

In silent songs, where laughter thins,
The wilds enchant with silly spins.
Each chuckle echoes through the glen,
Joyful tunes for all now and then!

Verses Swept Away by the Breeze

Through gentle winds, the grasses sway,
A wise old tree began to play.
With leaves of laughter, rustling light,
It told of squirrels who danced all night!

The daisies whispered secrets bold,
Of how the sun was once big and gold.
They giggled when a breeze went past,
And sings of the past, made the moment last!

The butterflies shared tales of flight,
How they once scared a poor lad at night.
They painted skies with vibrant cheer,
And promised a journey, so sincere!

So let the breeze sweep worries away,
As nature plays in its merry way.
With verses spun in a cheeky trance,
Get lost in the joy of this wild dance!

Reflections from the Moorland Kingdom

In a kingdom of bogs and twists,
Where the sheep wear crowns of mist,
The king's lost his way to brunch,
But he'll find it if he just holds a hunch.

The rabbits hold court, they decree,
That carrots must dance with glee,
While the geese honk tales of dread,
Of socks so mismatched, they must be fed.

The wind plays tricks on my hat,
It's a high-flying acrobat!
And the flowers gossip with glee,
About the clumsy dwarf who tripped on a bee.

So here's to the tyrant of toad,
Who rests on a marshy road,
With a jester who juggles and flops,
While all the jokes just never stops!

Petals in the Whispering Wind

Petals fly with a giggle, so light,
In a dance that ignites pure delight,
The bees are buzzed about the show,
Claiming dew drops as drinks to bestow.

The lilacs laugh at the stubborn oak,
Whose branches bend, poor fellow, bespoke,
'Why can't you sway like we do?' they tease,
'Join our merry waltz 'neath the trees!'

A dandelion, proud with fluffy might,
Says, 'I'm a star in the breeze tonight!'
With a puff, it sends dreams to the moon,
While clovers hum a sweet, silly tune.

So let's frolic where petals converse,
In laughter that spins the universe,
For nature's more joyous, fun-filled affair,
Where every flower has stories to share!

Songs of the Forgotten Glade

In a glade where the squirrels calm sing,
The mushrooms wear caps, each a bling,
With echoes of laughter tumbling like gold,
Where even the shyest tree's stories unfold.

The brook, full of giggles and quick little hops,
Brings news of the crickets and bumblebee flops,
And the owl, who thinks he's a wise old sage,
Is caught with a worm in a very odd rage.

Daisies declare it's a fancy parade,
While petunias gossip—oh, how they cascade!
A raccoon in tux makes a clumsy start,
As laughter erupts from the wildflower's heart.

So let's dance in the mud, and be merry and free,
For life in the glade is a grand jubilee,
With each note of nature, a humorous jive,
In the whispers of wild where we come alive!

Notes from the Wildflower's Heart

In a meadow where laughter is sown,
Wildflowers boast of their colors alone,
They twirl in the breeze, each petal ablaze,
While bragging of bees and flouncy bouquets.

The daisies debate who's best in the sun,
While the tulips cheer, 'We've also got fun!'
The thistle pipes up with a prickly charm,
'Watch out for me, I can provide an alarm.'

The butterflies flutter with skirts that dazzle,
Each twist and twirl, a whimsical razzle.
They gossip of crickets who dance on a dime,
While crafting shy sonnets in delicate rhyme.

So come join the choir of riotous blooms,
Where laughter and nectar weave into plumes,
In the notes of the wildflower's carefree jest,
You'll find that the silly is truly the best!

Serenade of the Sapphire Sky

Up high, the clouds do prance,
Chasing dreams in a vast expanse.
A pigeon sings a cheeky tune,
While bees dance beneath the moon.

The sun wears shades, oh what a sight,
Winking at us, feeling just right.
Birds gossip in a feathery flare,
As squirrels juggle without a care.

A kite slips away, tied to a man,
Who yells, "Come back!" like a windswept fan.
The trees laugh at his tangled fight,
While stars peek out, twinkling bright.

As day in laughter begins to fade,
The stars in rhythm, a cozy parade.
With giggles and snickers, the moon joins in,
Tonight's a riot, let the fun begin!

A Quest for the Celestial Flower

Once there lived a forgetful knight,
Whose sword was lost in a grand old fight.
In search of blooms that shine and glisten,
He even asked a squirrel to listen.

Down in the woods, a rabbit danced,
With carrots in hand, his chance enhanced.
"Looking for petals, you silly chap?
Try the bakery; they have quite the flap!"

Through meadows and brooks, he blundered and roamed,
Chasing butterflies, feeling quite home.
"Is that a flower or a colorful sock?
Oh wait, it's the bottom of my old frock!"

At last he found blooms, so bright and merry,
Only to trip on a prickly berry.
The quest was funny, with laughter and cheer,
A knight with a flower, that's the best career!

The Tapestry of Thistle Dreams

In a garden filled with dreams, so spry,
A hedgehog juggled, oh my, oh my!
With daisies as weights, what a rare sight,
While butterflies giggle in sheer delight.

A thistle declared, "I'm the queen of the show!"
While daisies rolled their eyes in a row.
"Your pointy crown, it's quite ostentatious!
But your dance moves are truly audacious!"

In the shade, a turtle wore sunglasses cool,
Sipping on nectar like a charming fool.
"I'll nap while you twirl, bright blooms on their feet,
Wake me when it's time for a scrumptious treat!"

Yet laughter echoed through the floral maze,
As friends joined in for a prance and a gaze.
In thistles and dreams, the fun had no seam,
For friendship blooms in the wildest dream!

Cadence of the Purple Horizon

As the sun sets in a purple flare,
A cat strums chords, hanging in mid-air.
With a hat on his head, and shades on his nose,
He's the coolest feline that anyone knows.

The crickets tap dance to the evening tune,
While fireflies twinkle, lighting the room.
"Dance, you silly stars, don't be so shy,
Join us now, oh my, oh my!"

A penguin in flip-flops waddles on through,
Looking for fish and a dance floor too.
"Who can resist this rhythm so sweet?
Let's shimmy and shake to the night's heart beat!"

The horizon blushes, sharing the jest,
A world full of laughter, who'd have guessed?
As night wraps us up in its cozy embrace,
Let's giggle and dance, in this silly space!

Reveries of the purple Horizon

On the hill where the sheep like to graze,
There's a purple cloud that likes to laze.
It throws shadows on the daisies bright,
   As if to say, 'Let's party tonight!'

The sun dips low, in a golden splash,
While rabbits hop 'round in a funny dash.
A frog in a tux sings quite a tune,
Underneath a big, laughing moon.

The breeze dresses up in a polka dot gown,
As it twirls and spins, making the flowers frown.
"Oh dear!" they gasp, "What a comical sight!"
They dance and they giggle till deep in the night.

So here's to those hills, where the fun never wanes,
And laughter floats on like sweet candy canes.
In reverie red, they squirm and they play,
In this whimsical world, let us dream away.

Murmurs of Nature's Palette

Colors collide in a delightful mess,
Where squirrels wear capes, oh what a dress!
The bluebirds chirp as they try to paint,
A masterpiece while looking quite quaint.

Paint pots spill over with hues of surprise,
As worms in bow ties perform acrobatics in skies.
The daisies are giggling, they just can't keep still,
While butterflies zoom in wild and free will.

"Look at me!" croaks a wise old frog,
Who leaps and then trips over a log.
The daisies roll over with laughter so bright,
In the quirky dance of the day and the night.

So let nature draw sketches with a splash and a cheer,
Where every stroke makes the oddness quite clear.
In the canvas of life, we've nothing to fret,
Just giggles and chuckles, you'll never forget.

Echoes Under the Dancing Sun

Beneath the sun, where the daisies sway,
A lizard in glasses declares, "Hip hooray!"
The shadows do jazz, what a raucous scene,
While flowers giggle in their best green sheen.

The wind starts to whistle a silly refrain,
And clouds float around like they're going insane.
A butterfly yells, "Hey, I'm here for the fun!"
As ants throw a party beneath the warm sun.

In the distance, a goat starts a drumroll,
As flowers erupt in a flash mob stroll.
"Let's shimmy and shake!" the petals all hum,
With bees doing flips, oh how they can run!

So join in the chaos of nature's grand scheme,
Where laughter erupts like a bright, bubbling stream.
Under the sun, with its rays so divine,
Life's a fantastic show, and the stars will align.

Bard of the Blooms and Mists

There once was a bard who sang to the blooms,
In a garden where laughter filled all the rooms.
His lute was a cucumber, his hat made of grass,
He crooned to the flowers as the butterflies passed.

The roses do a tango, the tulips can twist,
While daisies confetti with each bouncy fist.
"More fun!" sings the bard, with a wink and a smile,
As the violets giggle, they're dancing in style.

Mist swirls around, like a playful ghost,
As crickets take turns to buzz and to boast.
"It's grand in the glen!" they all holler and cheer,
As the bard spins around, "Let's dance through the year!"

So raise up your hands, full of petals and joy,
In this festival of nature, no one can annoy.
With blooms all enchanted in this magical mist,
Join the bard's crazy song, you simply can't resist!

Whispers of Distant Mountain Flowers

In the heights where daisies laugh,
A bee lost its way, a silly gaffe.
Petals dance, making a fuss,
While ants march on, driven by bus.

Sunbeams tickle the blooming thyme,
While butterflies drink some wild lime.
A squirrel glares at a passing kite,
Claiming the skies are his birthright.

Clouds giggle over the mountain range,
As shadows twist, humor's the change.
With each breeze the flowers sing,
Their banter makes the insects swing.

Laughter echoes through the green halls,
Where nature plays and merriment sprawls.
Underneath a tree that creaks,
The mountain whispers its funny peaks.

Hymns of the Nature's Trellis

Winding vines hum in the breeze,
While crickets hop like they own the keys.
A chipmunk plots an acorn spree,
With plans that stretch to eternity.

Tulips gossip with their glowing heads,
As sunflowers nod, sharing their threads.
Each blossom claims the quirkiest pet,
In gardens where buddies don't fret.

The wind lifts leaves for a fleeting dance,
As rabbits hop, they spin and prance.
Amongst the greens, the tales unfold,
With laughter rich, in sunlight bold.

Mossy carpets cushion the fall,
As ants debate the best snack call.
Listen closely, hear the jokes,
In nature's thrum, it surely pokes.

The Quietude of the Verdant Wilds

In tranquil woods where whispers play,
The trees are jesters at end of day.
Squirrels giggle, making a scene,
Chasing shadows, they're rather keen.

Beneath a bush, a rabbit sits,
Shuffling through leaves, sharing its wits.
A wise old owl fluffs its feathers bright,
Saying, "Life's funny—oh, what a fright!"

Blades of grass tickle the soles,
While frogs croak their rhythmic goals.
Nature's choir sounds quite absurd,
With how the songs are deftly blurred.

As dusk unfolds with a cheeky grin,
Fireflies begin their flickering spin.
The wilds engage in a flawless jest,
Welcoming all to nature's fest.

Enchanted Lullabies from the Woodlands

In dreamy woods where moonlight streams,
The night sings softly, mingling dreams.
Owls recite their tales with flair,
While hedgehogs giggle in their lair.

Bats swoop low with playful speed,
While underbrush rustles, oh what a lead!
A firefly winks, wanting attention,
Drawing shadows in light's invention.

Branches sway with a gentle tease,
As crickets tap dance, doing as they please.
The wind whispers jokes to passing deer,
A woodland comedy, oh so dear!

Stars twinkle in high places above,
Reflecting on nature's silliest love.
And as the night carries its tune,
The forest chuckles under the moon.

Serenade of the Lone Skylark

In the sky, a bird sings loud,
A lark on high, feeling proud.
Wings flapping, it does a dance,
Each note's a funny little chance.

Silly shadows on the ground,
Chasing giggles all around.
With a wiggle and a twirl,
It turns the moor into a whirl.

A plump rabbit joins the tune,
Bouncing along beneath the moon.
Together they strut in style,
With goofy grins that stretch a mile.

The sun dips low, the day does end,
With a laugh, the lark ascends.
In this jest, the night is spun,
Where every joke has just begun.

Starlit Echoes from the Moor

Under stars, the grass does sway,
Whispers of fun, come out to play.
Crickets chirp a quirky song,
In moonlit laughter, they belong.

A hedgehog rolls, all spiked and round,
In muddy puddles, it's quite the clown.
With a snicker at the moonlight's glow,
It trips and tumbles, oh what a show!

The owls hoot, a comical cheer,
For the antics they see, they hold dear.
While frogs croak jokes that never tire,
In this moorland night, we conspire.

Laughter ripples through the breeze,
Nature's humor puts hearts at ease.
As stars twinkle in the vast expanse,
The echoes of joy make us dance.

Eternal Songs of the Faraway Fields

Fields of daisies greet the dawn,
With a giggle, the day is drawn.
Butterflies flit, all dressed so bright,
A fashion show in morning light.

Cows chew cud, oh what a sight,
Munching grass with sheer delight.
The farmer's hat, it takes a dive,
Chased by wind, what a silly vibe!

Sunflowers sway with golden grins,
As the day spins on, the fun begins.
Pigs roll 'round in a muddy pool,
Creating chaos, their favorite rule.

As the sun takes its final bow,
Fields whisper secrets, here and now.
In every corner, joy's unfurled,
These songs of laughter shape our world.

Ballads Born in Colorful Hues

Crayons dance upon the page,
Painting stories, all the rage.
Rainbow hues, they laugh and play,
In their colorful, cheeky way.

A blue dog plays loud tunes with glee,
While polka dots jump, wild and free.
With red balloons that tickle clouds,
The joy within just laughs out loud.

Swirls of orange, a cheeky glance,
From vivid fields, we take a chance.
In the garden of laughs, we find,
A canvas where we're intertwined.

So let the colors sing their song,
In this funny world, we belong.
Each hue a giggle waiting to burst,
In ballads bright, we quench our thirst.

Rhymes from the Blooms of Loneliness

In the garden where daisies grow,
A squirrel lost his favorite show.
He searched for snacks, oh what a plight,
But found only weeds in the fading light.

The roses giggled, all in a bunch,
As the sunlight fell on their crunchy lunch.
A sunflower danced, did a silly twirl,
While the daisies laughed, giving each a whirl.

A snail, so slow, made a grand jest,
Claiming he was simply the best dressed.
With a shell that shimmered, oh so bright,
He'd charm the clouds, much to their delight.

But when raindrops fell, a quirk occurred,
All the flowers laughed, their humor stirred.
They dodged the drops like kiddies at play,
In the blooms of loneliness, joy led the way.

Whispers of the Rolling Lavender

In fields of purple, whispers twirl,
Where bees buzz on in a dizzy swirl.
A lavender hum, it tickles the bone,
Making everyone dance, even a stone!

The bumblebees wear tiny hats,
While butterflies gossip about silly chats.
They claim the sun is far too bright,
As they hide beneath blooms to laugh at the sight.

A rabbit hops, with feet so spry,
Chasing the shadows, oh my, oh my!
He trips on a stem, falls with a bump,
And the flowers cackle, oh what a thump!

Yet through the laughter, there's sweetness found,
In blooms that gather 'round the ground.
The rolling lavender holds a surprise,
When life is a jest, see it through bright eyes.

Songs from the Untamed Hills

Up in the hills, where wild things prance,
A goat on a rock starts a merry dance.
He wiggles his horns to an old folks' tune,
As coyotes join in, under the moon!

With every leap, a chuckle erupts,
As sheep in a line all hiccup and jump.
The daisies look on, shaking their heads,
While grasshoppers leap on their tiny beds.

A hedgehog croons with a voice so sweet,
It makes even mountains tap their feet.
He sings of the bugs that he'd like to meet,
And all the green things that taste like a treat.

The untamed hills echo with their glee,
As laughter rolls like a wild, bouncy spree.
Where nature's jesters give life a spin,
In the songs of the hills, let the fun begin!

Harmonies of the Scottish Ruins

In ancient stones where laughter rings,
A bagpipe player forgets his strings.
With a wink at the crowd, he plays a tune,
That makes the mice dance under the moon.

The castle walls echo with jovial cries,
As a wispy ghost playfully flies.
He twirls in the air, both cheeky and spry,
Taunting the tourists as they pass by.

A cat on the prowl strikes a silly pose,
Pretending to be royalty, held by her nose.
With a flick of her tail, she dons a crown,
In the ruins, every head must bow down!

Yet in these stones, filled with jest and cheers,
History chuckles and wipes away tears.
In the Scottish ruins, tales intertwine,
Where laughter persists like the best bottle of wine.

Melodic Tales of the Highland Glen

In the glen where bagpipes play,
The sheep dance in a cheeky ballet.
A haggis winks from its grassy throne,
Wishing it could scamper home alone.

The hills giggle with whispers of cheer,
As a cow starts to twirl, oh dear!
With a leap and a bound, it gives a shout,
Turning the quiet sheep inside out.

A squirrel wearing a tiny hat,
Proclaims, 'I'm the king, now where's my cat?'
But cats merely blink and look away,
In this joyous, quirky countryside ballet.

With every beat, the knees start to bend,
As the glen draws all to a laughable end.
So raise a toast to the silly and free,
In this merry Celtic jamboree!

An Ode to the Moorland Beauty

Upon the moor with a colorful tune,
A hedgehog's humor makes flowers swoon.
The bumblebees giggle, they're feeling bold,
    Stealing nectar like it's made of gold.

With a march of the ants and the dance of the breeze,
Around comes a fox, saying 'Just try to tease!'
He slips on a stone, gives a comical yell,
And the whole of the moor bursts into a swell.

The colors collide in a burst of delight,
As a llama strolls by, looking just right.
'What a fine day to play dress-up!' it says,
    Strutting around in a plaid with a haze.

As the sun starts to dip with a chuckle and wink,
The moorland's a stage, oh don't you think?
So let the stories of laughter unfold,
A joyful adventure in shades of bold!

Fragrance of the Rolling Heather

Rolling fields where the mischief lies,
A goat chews on grass, wearing silly ties.
The breezes carry a scent so sweet,
While rabbits gather for a daring feat.

In the distance, a llama attempts a leap,
While hedgehogs giggle and tumble in heaps.
With every misstep, the meadows rejoice,
For laughter is louder than any fine voice.

Daisies are dressed in their best morning glow,
As the daisies decide to put on a show.
They twirl and they swirl like tiny ballerinas,
While sunshine kisses the high-peaked arenas.

With the sun setting low and the giggles so grand,
Even the stones seem to wiggle and stand.
So here in this land of whimsy and cheer,
Let the fragrance of fun linger ever near!

Harmonies of the Wild Venturers

In the wild, they gather, the quirky of kin,
A badger in boots starts to spin and grin.
With each little blunder of skipping too far,
The owls chuckle along with a sparkly star.

The rabbits hold court, spinning tales of delight,
About chasing their shadows well into the night.
With a giggle and hop, they forget all their fears,
As the moon waves hello with a glimmer of cheers.

Not far from the brook, a frog dons a crown,
Singing songs of laughter while upside down.
Each splash sends ripples, a whimsical tune,
While stars in the sky rattle with mirth, like a cartoon.

As the wild venturers twirl 'neath the moon's glow,
Remember the fun in this world we bestow.
So dance with the breeze, and sing with the trees,
In this land filled with joy, let your spirit seize!

Ballad of the Blazing Heather

In fields where the wild flowers dance,
The bees hold a raucous romance.
They buzz with a swaggering flair,
Claiming sweet nectar without a care.

Yet here comes a goat with a grin,
He eats every petal with a spin.
"Hey mate, that's my lunch!" the bee shouts,
But the goat just laughs, he has no doubts.

A squirrel observes from a tree,
Thinking, "Such lunacy, let it be!"
He calculates all that he sees,
Then leaps for a berry, much to his ease.

So gather 'round, all who adore,
The laughter that nature can store.
With fauna and flora in jest,
It's a light-hearted life that we love best.

Lullabies of the Highlands

In the highlands where sheep graze wide,
One laments, "Where's my woolly bride?"
With a bleat that's more like a plea,
He searches the pastures so carefree.

A fox struts in with a knowing grin,
"Chill out, mate, you'll soon find kin!"
The sheep rolls his eyes, quite exasperated,
Counting his flock, slightly frustrated.

A dancing otter joins the play,
With splashes that make the sheep sway.
"Join the fun," he calls out loud,
But the sheep just sighs, lost in a cloud.

So under the stars, when shadows blend,
These creatures unite, laughter will send.
With a cuddle of mischief and cheer,
Highland tunes ring, delightful and clear.

The Velvet Whisper of Thistles

Amidst the thistles, sharp but proud,
A ladybug twirls, feeling loud.
With polka-dots and a sassy parade,
She claims the soft petals, unafraid.

A grasshopper sings from the shade,
"Hey, ladybug, join the charade!"
But a breeze sends thistles dancing fast,
It's a prickly partition, none can surpass.

The ladybug giggles, "Not in my style!"
She struts off with a confident smile.
While the thistles rustle, planning their jest,
"How do we blend in with the best?"

So in the meadows where colors collide,
Thistles and bugs take a wild ride.
In laughter or trouble, they find a way,
To dance in the chaos of a bright day.

Serenade of the Soft Breeze

A soft breeze whispers tales untold,
Tickling noses in the morning cold.
"Hey there, grass! Don't be so stiff,
It's time to sway, give nature a lift!"

The daisies laugh, swaying with glee,
"Come on, breeze, dance here with me!"
But the breeze teases, "I'm off for a flight,
To visit those flowers, oh what a sight!"

Butterflies flutter, chomping on cake,
"Hold steady, breeze, for goodness' sake!"
But the breeze just giggles with every flap,
Whisking off petals, making a trap.

So join the frolic, let the laughter ring,
With breezy melodies that joyously sing.
In a world where whimsy forever stays,
Embrace the humor in life's gentle plays.

Verses from the Fabled Glens

In valleys deep where trolls do laugh,
The trees all dance, they'd love a gaffe.
A squirrel stole my sandwich, oh what a crime,
Now I'm left with just pickles, a real tough time.

The river sings songs of ducks on parade,
They quack with style, in a grand charade.
A frog hops by, with a crown on tight,
Claiming he's king – what a silly sight!

Mossy rocks whisper secrets so bold,
Of ancient tales and treasures untold.
A rabbit winks, it's a cheeky tease,
With carrots that dance in a summer breeze.

So raise a glass to glens we adore,
With wild hearts and laughter galore.
For every ramble and every jest,
We'll find the fun in nature's quest.

Songs of the Lonely Expanse

Out in the fields where the daisies bloom,
A scarecrow pirouettes, banishing gloom.
The wind starts to hum, it's a catchy jive,
While ants march along with a confident vibe.

Clouds play hide and seek, oh what a game,
While sunbeams tickle – who's to blame?
A butterfly giggles in a flurry of colors,
Daring the bees to join in with others.

A distant cow moos a melodious tune,
As rabbits hop madly, endearing their swoon.
With every rustle, the chuckles arise,
In the expanse, we share in surprise.

Let's dance with shadows and leap with the breeze,
Make funny faces, do it with ease.
In open fields, let merriment spread,
For joy is a song, and we're all well-fed.

Echoes Across the Nature's Canvas

The mountains yodel in a rocky choir,
As goats on a ledge conspire and conspire.
A raccoon in shades steals cookies with flair,
While birds chirp gossip, floating in air.

Berries burst forth, a sweet juicy prank,
As deer prance about to a funky bank.
The sun – a spotlight on nature's grand show,
Where every creature steals the flow.

The wind tells tall tales of squirrels in suits,
While flowers debate about whom to recruit.
With laughter like raindrops, the joy overflows,
In this canvas of nature, humor bestows.

So paint it with giggles, brush with delight,
For every mischief makes the day bright.
With echoes of laughter, let it resound,
In the symphony of life, funny moments abound.

Romantic Laments of the Open Wilderness

The leaves crackle softly underfoot,
As I trip on my laces, what a cute hoot!
A porcupine flirts with a nearby tree,
But it's really just looking for lunch, you see.

The moon winks down, planning to joke,
As owls look on, but they never spoke.
A romantic fool on the edge of a stream,
Dreaming of chamomile tea and whipped cream.

A bear with a bowtie joins in the fun,
While bunnies debate who's faster to run.
It's a wilderness ball, with laughter we share,
Well, except for the moose—he's lost in his hair.

Underneath stars with their twinkling smiles,
We stumble through paths, and share silly styles.
In this wild romance, with giggles we roam,
Finding joy in the laughter that feels like home.

Rhapsody of the Whispering Greens

In fields where grass takes flight,
The ants all sing with delight.
They march in lines, a tiny parade,
With tiny hats that they have made.

The cows start mooing a quirky tune,
As butterflies dance beneath the moon.
A rabbit hops, then slips on dew,
Turns around and yells, "Who knew?"

Daisies sway and beg for prance,
While frogs decide to join the dance.
They leap and croak, a spectral choir,
As snails debate who's the true flyer.

The wind blows soft, a gentle jest,
Tickling flowers, giving them rest.
They giggle and chuckle, feeling spry,
As nature sings its lullaby.

Chants of the Unseen Meadows

Where daisies bloom with silly grins,
The caterpillars sing in spins.
They twist and twirl on silken threads,
Creating chaos, leaping heads.

Squirrels debate the best acorn,
While chipmunks argue, slightly worn.
They toss and turn, a comedic sight,
Who knew nature could be so light?

Bumblebees buzz in a light confusion,
Chasing shadows in wild delusion.
They zap and dart, in dizzy loops,
As frogs join in, oh, what a troupe!

The grasses chuckle, swaying with flair,
As sunshine paints everything rare.
In meadows vast, with laughter bright,
Every creature shares the delight.

Below the Boughs of Nature's Heart

Beneath the boughs where shadows play,
A raccoon shows off, in a sneaky way.
He juggles nuts, an act of skill,
While owls just stare, not a sound, until.

The squirrels cheer and clap their paws,
As chipmunks giggle, giving applause.
The old oak chuckles with a wise old creak,
"Just one more trick!" it seems to speak.

A mouse with dreams of becoming grand,
Pretends to dance with a tiny band.
The stars peek down through leafy lips,
As crickets join with their little quips.

And under stars that twinkle bright,
Creatures share stories late into night.
In this grove where laughter starts,
Nature shows her joyful heart.

The Singing Shadows on the Moor

On the moor where shadows blend,
The sheep hold concerts, no need to pretend.
They baa in harmony, a woolly choir,
As they prance about, fueled by desire.

The bumblebees buzz a funny refrain,
Each note a wobble, the humor's plain.
A hedgehog joins with a little spin,
As daisies giggle, caught in the din.

The stones start rolling, wanting a part,
In this epic tale of nature's art.
With laughter soaring across the glen,
Even the breezes play along again.

So raise a cheer for the moor's wild song,
Where nonsense reigns and laughter's strong.
In each crevice, a punchline awaits,
As nature celebrates, shedding its weights.

The Enchanted Air

In a land where the sheep wear fuzzy crowns,
The rabbits dance in their fluffy gowns.
A breeze carries whispers of old,
As the sun shines bright on tales untold.

Birds chirp gossip from tree to tree,
Claiming the sky is a bird's marquee.
With every flap, they share a jest,
In the enchanted air, all feel blessed.

Rhythms of the Highlands

A bagpipe's wail in the drizzly mist,
Makes even the trolls shake their fist.
With every note, the mountains sway,
As folks in kilts dance the day away.

The loch reflects the laughter clear,
While fish giggle softly — can you hear?
A jig on the grass, quite a sight,
Rhythms of the Highlands, pure delight!

Secrets Beneath the Purple Canopy

Under the blooms of violet bliss,
Squirrels gather for a nutty kiss.
They share secrets with butterflies,
While playing hide and seek from prying eyes.

A gnome peeks out with a cheeky grin,
As fairies giggle and twirl and spin.
In this realm where laughter thrives,
Secrets bloom like wildflower drives.

Hymns of the Rolling Hills

The rolling hills hum a merry tune,
As cows in the field dance under the moon.
They sway and moo to the farmer's delight,
While pigs roll in mud, what a sight!

A fox tries to join in the fun,
But trips over grass, oh, what's to be done?
In these hills where laughter spills,
We sing out loud, in joyful thrills!

Ballads of the Bountiful Meadow

In the meadow where cows dance,
A cowbell concerto starts to prance.
Sunflowers bow with a funny grace,
While rabbits hop in a wild race.

Bees wear hats, how dapper they hum,
While daisies gossip, oh so glum.
A pig in boots, oh what a sight,
In this bountiful place, all feels right.

A scarecrow sleeps, dreaming of fame,
While crows conspire to change his name.
They call him 'Sir Fluff' as they play,
In this joyful meadow, come what may.

Nature's jester with every sound,
In the laughter of blooms, pure joy is found.
Frolic and glee in each face you meet,
This meadow of mirth is life's upbeat.

Traces of the Mountain Air

Up in the hills, the squirrels do sing,
As chipmunks dance and the crickets zing.
With each gust, a tickle and tease,
The pines sway like they're in a breeze.

Goats wear ties, quite the classy crew,
While marmots play hide and seek for view.
A yodeler trips, oh what a slip,
As laughter echoes, nature's little quip.

Clouds like sheep pass by with a bleat,
As the sun pinches cheeks with warmth so sweet.
The mountain air whispers its jokes so rare,
These playful mischiefs are too good to bear.

Frolicking fairies hide behind rocks,
While council of owls chime in with knocks.
In this playful realm, all troubles flee,
With every trace of air, so carefree.

Celestial Chants of the Bog

In the bog where the frogs are bright,
They croak out tunes under moonlight.
With dragonflies zipping in a race,
This swampy stage is a silly place.

A snail with shades takes it slow,
While reeds tap dance to the bog's flow.
The sun sets low with a splash and a pop,
As critters gather for the evening hop.

Marshmallow mushrooms giggle with glee,
While owls throw jokes from each old tree.
The waters ripple with some sly grins,
In this quagmire of mirth, where fun begins.

Witty winks from the fireflies, blink,
While turtles play poker and others think.
Amidst this chaos, the moon's a grand host,
In this celestial bog, let's raise a toast.

Nocturne of the Whispering Winds

In the night, the wind starts to hum,
With whispers of tales from the olden drum.
Trees sway gently as they start to sway,
In a nocturne dance that's here to play.

Owls jest with riddles in a deep voice,
While shadows scatter, a sneaky choice.
A raccoon juggles acorns with flair,
In this whimsical night, joy fills the air.

The stars wink down, mischievous and bright,
As crickets strum soft songs of delight.
Moonbeams giggle on grass that sways,
In this night symphony, laughter stays.

So hush now, dear friends, and lend an ear,
To the winds that carry good cheer near.
In whispers of night, let the fun unfurl,
In this playful tune, welcome the world.

Harmonies of the Untrodden Pathways

Upon a route where no one goes,
A squirrel contorts, strikes silly poses.
A jig in the grass, a twirl with glee,
I laugh aloud, oh what a spree!

The view is grand, but wait—what's that?
A goat approaches, looking quite fat.
It bleats a tune, off-key and loud,
I join in chorus, feeling quite proud!

Behind the bushes, there's a dance
With wildflowers sharing their chance.
Petals all flutter, in blissful delight,
As I join the fray, twirling loose and tight.

Lost in this revel, I lose my way,
But who cares! It's a glorious day.
With laughter echoed in the breeze,
In my heart, I feel the tease!

Memories of the Highland Blooms

In fields where daisies have all their say,
I trip on roots, start to sway.
A tumble here, a roll or two,
The flowers chuckle, and so do you.

The bees are buzzing with gossiping glee,
Whispering secrets to each flower tree.
A tumbleweed rolls like it's on a spree,
Enticing my legs to join the spree.

Jellybean clouds drift and tease my hair,
While I dance with trolls without a care.
With every misstep comes a laugh so bright,
In this land of flowers, everything's right.

Memories grow in this wild ballet,
With petals brightening my silly fray.
So lift your voice, let laughter loom,
In this garden where giggles bloom!

Rhythms of the Ethereal Meadow

In a meadow where giggles float high,
The sky is a canvas, laughter shall fly.
Butterflies waltz, there's glee in each flap,
While I dance wildly, a graceful mishap!

There's a rabbit who hops like it's all a game,
Lost in the rhythm, we're never the same.
Round and around, we twist and shout,
While daisies tap toes and join in the clout.

A lone frog croaks a most dreadful tune,
Yet magic hangs lightly, like dust from the moon.
With each clumsy step, the meadow's ablaze,
In this whimsical world, we skip and we gaze.

Lost in this dream of frolic and fun,
We tango with daisies, oh what a run!
In the rhythms of laughter, we find our place,
In the quirky embrace of this joyous space!

Celebrations of the Highland's Bounty

With a basket of berries and giggles in store,
Off to the hills for a feast and more.
A raccoon appears, quite the cunning chap,
Swiping my snacks while I'm all agape!

"Come join the feast!" I shout in delight,
But it scampers away in the soft twilight.
The laughter spills over like jam on bread,
While I dub it a fine meal—though candy instead!

Wildflowers join, in a colorful cheer,
Celebrating life with every bright dear.
So here's to the snacks, and those that beg,
And to raccoons who dance with their loads on a leg!

Let's raise a toast to this merry plight,
With honey and berries, oh what a sight!
In the heart of the highlands, let joy count the cost,
In these celebrations, we see what's not lost!

Soliloquy of the Wandering Wilds

In the woods where shadows play,
A squirrel steals my lunch today.
He twirls around, so full of cheer,
I'm just a guest, while he's the peer.

Amid the blooms, I lost my shoes,
Now I wander in mismatched hues.
A rabbit laughs, his ears so tall,
While I trip over a carelessly fallen ball.

The trees gossip, with leaves to sway,
I ask for wisdom, but they sway away.
Caterpillars with monocles stare,
As if judging my lack of flair.

At dusk, the crickets start to sing,
While I just dance, a clumsy fling.
Nature chuckles, gives me a nod,
How wild it is to dance with odd!

Lyrics in the Misty Heaths

Amidst the mist, a hare sings low,
His voice is deep, but moves like snow.
I clap along, but trip on roots,
End up tangled in golden shoots.

Fog rolls in with a ghostly grin,
I play peek-a-boo, but lose my skin.
The daisies laugh, with petals wide,
As I chase after the misty tide.

A lark arrives with tales to tell,
Of whimsical winds in its airy shell.
But I trip on air, knock over a gnome,
Who shakes his fist, "This is my home!"

As the sun sets, I take a bow,
Cheers erupt from the bees somehow.
Nature's concert, with tunes so spry,
All I need is a good pair of shoes to fly!

Reverie of the Natural Kingdom

Upon the hill, the daisies hum,
While bunnies dance, and my heart goes thrum.
I tried to shout, but whispers slip,
They giggle at my failing trip.

The clover crowns a wise old snail,
Who speaks in rhymes, yet leaves a trail.
With every note, I join the spree,
But ants remind me, I'm not so free.

At twilight's call, the fireflies waltz,
While I fumble, but who really faults?
Flowers grin, with petals so bright,
"Just join the fun, it's quite alright!"

A chorus grows, with frogs in tow,
They ribbit alive, with a lively flow.
I laugh along, in this vast delight,
In nature's arms, whimsy takes flight!

The Dance of the Purple Blossoms

In fields of purple, the giggles swell,
With butterflies spinning a funny spell.
I join the dance, but lose my way,
As bees join in for a wild ballet.

The blossoms twirl, in breezy delight,
Chasing my hat, it takes to flight.
A comedic chase, my clumsiness plain,
While daisies chuckle at my disdain.

A ladybug winks from her throne,
As I trip again, I'm not alone.
The blooms all sway, they clap their leaves,
"Just keep it silly, or no reprieves!"

With every step, my shoes go 'pop',
As I pirouette, and nearly stop.
In laughter's grip, I find my glee,
Dancing in petals, forever carefree!

The Spirit of the Blooming Bracken

In fields where ferns in fashion sway,
The critters dance, come out to play.
A rabbit hops, a squirrel prances,
While daisies join in leafy glances.

The breeze does tickle tufted grass,
As ants conduct their tiny mass.
A frog croaks loud, a tune of cheer,
"Join me all! The party's here!"

With every leaf that rustles near,
The woodland chuckles, joy sincere.
The bracken whispers ancient lore,
Of laughter shared forevermore.

A hedgehog dons a tiny hat,
Proclaims himself, "Your party brat!"
So gather round, embrace the fun,
The spirit of the bracken's spun!

Ode to the Endless Pastures

In fields so green, where grasses twirl,
The sheep form bands, all in a swirl.
They bleat a tune, oh what a sight,
A woolly rave, from day to night!

The cows join in with mooing flair,
As daisies sway without a care.
With windblown hats, the flowers sing,
"Let's frolic now, it's springtime's fling!"

A playful goat jumps high and far,
He lands on a haystack, like a star!
The pastures echo with laughter bright,
As critters party under starlight.

With frolicsome hearts and joy that's free,
The meadow hosts a jubilee.
So raise a glass, and take a chance,
In endless pastures, let's all dance!

Reflections in the Misty Vale

In valleys deep, where fog does cling,
The willows sway, making hearts sing.
A foggy mix of giggles loud,
As frogs in chorus, form a crowd.

The ghostly trees share silly tales,
Of windy nights and wayward gales.
With spidery webs and fairy winks,
The mist reveals what nature thinks.

A playful pup runs through the haze,
Chasing shadows in mysterious ways.
While twinkling stars give quiet hope,
Glow-in-the-dark, the snails elope.

In reflections mild, the magic's clear,
The vale embraces fun and cheer.
So join the frolic, come what may,
In misty laughter, let's all play!

The Dance of the Moorland Spirits

In moorlands wide, where breezes swoop,
The spirits gather, a merry troupe.
With twinkling eyes, they start to prance,
Inviting all to join their dance.

A hare tiptoes with grace so sly,
While hares fly past, like clouds in sky.
The gorse erupts in golden glee,
As merry fairies sip their tea.

The rocks play drums, the sky spins round,
As laughter echoes, joy unbound.
With every leap, a joke delivered,
In moorland fun, we're all considered!

The spirits twirl, their song distinct,
As nature winks and winks, we think.
So join the dance, this merry quest,
In moorland spirits, we're truly blessed!

Rhythms of the Blossoming Heath

In a field where flowers sway,
A bumblebee forgot his way.
He danced upon a vibrant bloom,
Declaring, "This is my living room!"

A rabbit wearing tiny shoes,
Joined the party with his moves.
He wiggled and he hopped around,
While humming to the buzzing sound.

The daisies giggled, oh so loud,
As blooms swayed, making them proud.
They whispered jokes of sun and rain,
While butterflies flew by, insane!

Together all, in colors bright,
Held a festival of pure delight.
With laughter ringing through the air,
Each petal showed how much they care.

Melodies Amidst the Heather Blooms

A clownfish tried to wear a hat,
But slipped and fell upon a mat.
The daisies chuckled, blooms ablaze,
As everyone watched him in a daze.

The grasshoppers held an opera show,
Singing to the clouds, all in a row.
They tripped on tunes, their legs so spry,
While all of nature stopped to sigh.

A snail, with flair, began to glide,
Sassy as ever, full of pride.
His shell adorned with glittery glue,
He slipped right past a startled crew.

And when the sun began to fall,
The nightingale began to call.
In the concert of the woodland stage,
The wildflowers broke out in rage!

Echoes in the Highland Mist

Fog rolled in on tiptoes sly,
An owl blinked, thought he could fly.
He hooted jokes from high above,
While hugs of mist embraced the love.

Cows in plaid were playing cards,
While sheep in stripes just laughed, how hard!
They bet their wool on who could dance,
And twirled about in a silly trance.

The trees held gossip, soft and low,
About the fox who stole the show.
With bushy tail and tricky ways,
He pranced around, igniting praise.

As dawn creaked in, the laughter soared,
Each creature looked at life, adored.
With every echo, jokes set free,
The mist dissolved in joyful glee.

Verse of the Wildflower Breeze

The wildflowers wrote a silly song,
They danced and twirled all day long.
The breeze took notes and laughed out loud,
While clouds around formed a fluffy crowd.

A lurking cat tried to join the fun,
But tangled up in grass, oh what a run!
With paws all lost in petals wide,
He tumbled down, full of wild pride.

A butterfly, a diva fierce,
Flipped through colors, each petal pierce.
She struck a pose on golden tips,
While honeybees laid tunes on their lips.

And when the afternoon was bright,
The sun joined in, a bold delight.
With every laugh and whispered tease,
The wildflowers danced in a joyful breeze.

Reflections on the Blooming Earth

In a garden, the daisies dance,
Chasing bees in a rompy trance.
Tulips giggle in the sun,
While dandelions yell, "We're so much fun!"

The roses blush, oh what a fright,
Lustrous petals too shy for the light.
Lilies laugh at the passing ants,
Sipping nectar, they do little prance.

A sunflower grins, tall and proud,
Tiptoeing in tune with the cloud.
But when raindrops start to fall,
It's a slippery slide for them all!

As the moon blooms over the lot,
Worms tell tales of the mess they've got.
Each petal a giggle, a charming play,
In this blooming earth, we laugh all day!

Twilight Songs of the Wildflower Kingdom

Underneath the twinkling skies,
The wildflowers hum with sly surprise.
Buttercups sway to the crickets' beat,
While bees bust out their funky feet.

Bluebells chime, it's their time to sing,
Bringing laughter as they swing.
Poppies poke each other's fluff,
"Don't be shy, let's call this bluff!"

With twilight's breeze, a joke takes flight,
A nightingale makes the darkness bright.
"Who's that prancing in the night?
Careful now, or you'll lose your height!"

In the kingdom of blooms, hilarity reigns,
Where silly blooms face off with their gains.
A raucous show beneath the stars,
Moonlit giggles are never far!

Poetry Among the Whispering Breezes

Whispers flutter through the leaves,
Between the branches, mischief weaves.
A daisy declares, "My rhyme's the best!"
While a tulip teases, "I'm dressed to impress!"

Breezes carry the laughter wide,
As flower-friends play and glide.
Clover patches chuckle along,
Sharing giggles in a breezy song.

Rosemary jests with a foxglove's ring,
"I can smell trouble; let's take wing!"
They twirl in circles, a floral affair,
Chasing wind, without a care.

In this poetry of nature's jest,
Every bloom knows it's for the best.
With laughter sprouting from each crease,
The world spins round in hilarious peace!

Harmonies of the Majestic Tundra

In the tundra where the cold winds roll,
Lichens laugh, "We're on a stroll!"
Mossy patches crack silly grins,
"Don't freeze now, let the fun begin!"

Snowflakes flutter, a dance so rare,
Drifting softly through frosty air.
The tundra critters scamper and play,
Sliding and tumbling in their own ballet.

Icicles chime like giddy bells,
Sharing secrets in frosty swells.
"Who will catch a snowball today?
Just watch out, or you'll slip away!"

In this majestic realm, bright and bold,
Nature's laughter, never cold.
Each flake and twig sings a tune,
Revealing joy beneath the moon!

www.ingramcontent.com/pod-product-compliance
Lightning Source LLC
Chambersburg PA
CBHW051629160426
43209CB00004B/579